My State
SOUTH DAKOTA

By Christina Earley

TABLE OF CONTENTS

A Crabtree Seedlings Book

Crabtree Publishing
crabtreebooks.com

T0020327

School-to-Home Support for Caregivers and Teachers

This book helps children grow by letting them practice reading. Here are a few guiding questions to help the reader build his or her comprehension skills. Possible answers appear in red.

Before Reading:

• What do I know about South Dakota?
  • *I know that South Dakota is a state.*
  • *I know that South Dakota has plains.*

• What do I want to learn about South Dakota?
  • *I want to learn which famous people were born in South Dakota.*
  • *I want to learn what the state flag looks like.*

During Reading:

• What have I learned so far?
  • *I have learned that Pierre is the state capital of South Dakota.*
  • *I have learned that Mount Rushmore National Memorial was started in 1927 and finished in 1941.*

• I wonder why...
  • *I wonder why the state flower is the American pasque.*
  • *I wonder why the state sport is rodeo.*

After Reading:

• What did I learn about South Dakota?
  • *I have learned that you can watch basketball games at the Corn Palace.*
  • *I have learned that the state animal is the coyote.*

• Read the book again and look for the glossary words.
  • *I see the word **capital** on page 6, and the word **rodeo** on page 13. The other glossary words are found on pages 22 and 23.*

SOUTH DAKOTA

Hi! My name is Jayce. Welcome to South Dakota!

3

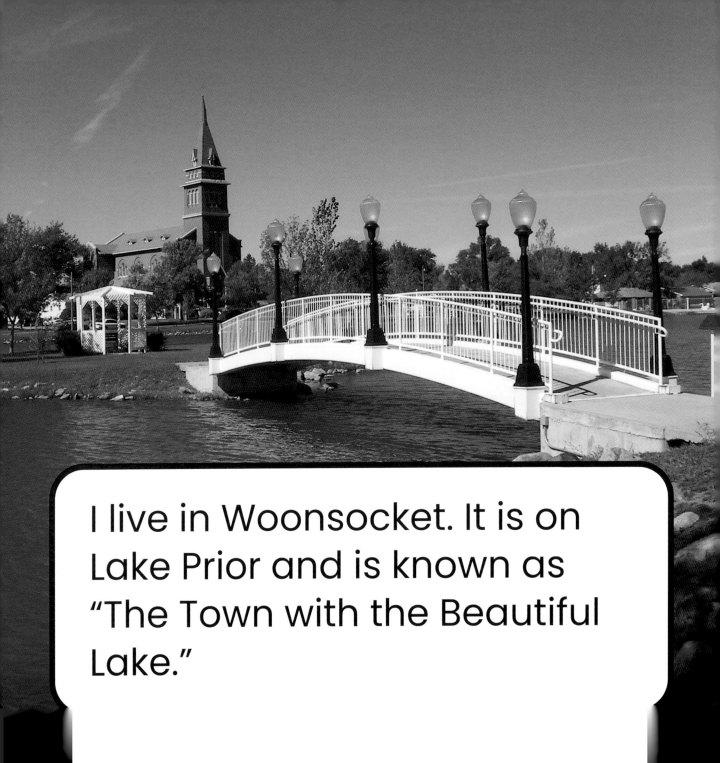

I live in Woonsocket. It is on Lake Prior and is known as "The Town with the Beautiful Lake."

We grow a lot of watermelons in Woonsocket.

Pierre

South Dakota is in the **midwestern** United States. The **capital** is Pierre.

Fun Fact: Sioux Falls is the largest city in South Dakota.

The state animal is the coyote.

The American pasque is the state flower.

We grow a lot of corn in South Dakota. Some of it is used to make corn muffins.

Fun Fact: South Dakota grows around 6.1 million tons (5.5 million metric tons) of corn a year.

My state flag is blue. The
state **seal** is in the middle.

Rodeo is the state sport.

I like to visit Mount Rushmore National **Memorial**. The faces of four U.S. presidents are **carved** into Mount Rushmore.

Fun Fact: Mount Rushmore National Memorial was started in 1927 and finished in 1941.

14

It is exciting to watch basketball games at the Corn Palace.

Baseball manager Sparky Anderson was born in South Dakota. Actress January Jones was also born in South Dakota.

Fun Fact: Stephanie Herseth Sandlin, the first woman from South Dakota elected to the U.S. House of Representatives, was born in Houghton, South Dakota.

I enjoy camping at Sylvan Lake.

Glossary

capital (cap-ih-tuhl): The city or town where the government of a country, state, or province is located

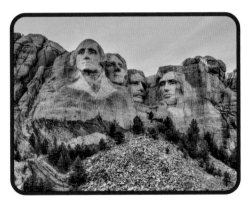

carve (karv): To create something, such as a sculpture, by cutting into and removing pieces of the material it is made of

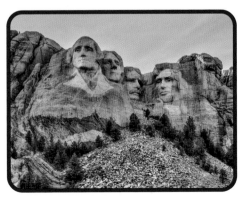

memorial (muh-mohr-ee-uhl): Something, such as a monument, that honors a person who is dead